Presented to:

_____

From:

_____

Date:

_____

Jesus Calling®

50 Devotions for

Encouragement

Sarah Young

THOMAS NELSON
Since 1798

Published in Nashville, Tennessee, by Thomas Nelson. Thomas Nelson is a registered trademark of HarperCollins Christian Publishing, Inc.

Unless otherwise noted, Scripture quotations are taken from the Holy Bible, New International Version®, niv®. Copyright © 1973, 1978, 1984 by Biblica, Inc.® Used by permission of Zondervan. All rights reserved worldwide. www.zondervan.com. The "niv" and "New International Version" are trademarks registered in the United States Patent and Trademark Office by Biblica, Inc.®

Scripture quotations marked amp are from the Amplified® Bible. Copyright © 1954, 1958, 1962, 1964, 1965, 1987 by The Lockman Foundation. Used by permission. (www.Lockman.org)

Scripture quotations marked kjv are from the King James Version. Public domain.

Scripture quotations marked nasb are from New American Standard Bible®. Copyright © 1960, 1962, 1963, 1968, 1971, 1972, 1973, 1975, 1977, 1995 by The Lockman Foundation. Used by permission. (www.Lockman.org)

Scripture quotations marked nkjv are from the New King James Version®. © 1982 by Thomas Nelson. Used by permission. All rights reserved.

Any Internet addresses, phone numbers, or company or product information printed in this book are offered as a resource and are not intended in any way to be or to imply an endorsement by Thomas Nelson, nor does Thomas Nelson vouch for the existence, content, or services of these sites, phone numbers, companies, or products beyond the life of this book.

ISBN 978-1-4003-1092-0

The Library of Congress has cataloged the earlier edition as follows:

Young, Sarah, 1946–
Jesus Calling / by Sarah Young.
p. cm.
ISBN 978-1-59145-188-4 (hardcover)
1. Devotional calendars. 2. Devotional literature, English. I. Title.
BV4811.Y675 2004
242'.2—dc22   2044005474

Printed in China

18 19 20 21 22 TIMS 5 4 3 2 1

Introduction

A sense of closeness to Jesus is perhaps the most important benefit to be found through the practice of being still in His Presence and making quiet reflection a priority. Another benefit of this is relief from stress and anxiety. You can ask Jesus to help you see things—including your problems—from His perspective.

The devotions in this book are meant to be read slowly, preferably in a quiet place—with your Bible open. The Bible is the only infallible, inerrant Word of God, and I endeavor to keep my writings consistent with that unchanging standard. I have written from the perspective of Jesus speaking, to help readers feel more personally connected with Him. So the first person singular ("I," "Me," "My," "Mine") always refers to Christ; "you" refers to you, the reader. Scripture references are included after each daily reading. Words from the Scriptures (some paraphrased, some quoted) are indicated in italics.

My prayer is that the Lord will continue to bless, help, strengthen, comfort, and encourage readers. It's so encouraging to know that you never face anything alone!

Sarah Young

I AM A MIGHTY GOD. *Nothing is too difficult for Me.* I have chosen to use weak ones like you to accomplish My purposes. Your weakness is designed to open you up to My Power. Therefore, do not fear your limitations or measure the day's demands against your strength. What I require of you is to stay connected to Me, living in trusting dependence on My limitless resources. When you face unexpected demands, there is no need to panic. Remember that *I am with you.* Talk with Me, and listen while I talk you through each challenging situation.

I am not a careless God. When I allow difficulties to come into your life, I equip you fully to handle them. Relax in My Presence, trusting in My Strength.

LUKE 1:37; DEUTERONOMY 31:8; 2 CORINTHIANS 12:9

The LORD *himself* goes before you and will be with you; he will *never* leave you nor forsake you. Do not be afraid; do not be discouraged.

—DEUTERONOMY 31:8

Continue on this path with Me, enjoying My Presence even in adversity. I am always before you, as well as alongside you. See Me beckoning to you: "Come! Follow Me." The One who goes ahead of you, opening up the way, is the same One who stays close and never lets go of your hand. I am not subject to limitations of time or space. I am everywhere at every time, ceaselessly working on your behalf. That is why your best efforts are trusting Me and living close to Me.

Isaiah 41:10 nasb; Hebrews 7:25; Psalm 37:3–4

"Do not fear, for I am with you; do not *anxiously* look about you, for I am your God. I will *strengthen* you, surely I will help you, surely I will uphold you with My *righteous* right hand."

—ISAIAH 41:10 NASB

I AM WITH YOU AND FOR YOU. When you decide on a course of action that is in line with My will, nothing in heaven or on earth can stop you. You may encounter many obstacles as you move toward your goal, but don't be discouraged—never give up! With My help, you can overcome any obstacle. Do not expect an easy path as you journey hand in hand with Me, but do remember that I, your *very-present Helper*, am omnipotent.

Much, much stress results from your wanting to make things happen before their times have come. One of the main ways I assert My sovereignty is in the timing of events. If you want to stay close to Me and do things My way, ask Me to show you the path forward moment by moment. Instead of dashing headlong toward your goal, let Me set the pace. Slow down, and enjoy the journey in My Presence.

ROMANS 8:31; PSALM 46:1–3 NKJV; LUKE 1:37

What, then,

shall we say in

response

to this? If God is

for us, who can be

against us?

—ROMANS 8:31

GROW STRONG in the Light of My Presence. As My Face shines upon you, you receive nutrients that enhance your growth in grace. I designed you to commune with Me face to Face, and this interaction strengthens your soul. Such communion provides a tiny glimpse of what awaits you in heaven, where all barriers between you and My Glory will be removed. This meditative time with Me blesses you doubly: You experience My Presence here and now, and you are refreshed by the hope of heaven, where you will know Me in ecstatic Joy.

PSALM 4:6–8; REVELATION 21:23; 2 PETER 3:13

Many are asking, "Who can show us any good?" Let the *light* of your face shine upon us, O Lord. You have filled my heart with greater *joy* than when their grain and new wine abound. I will lie down and sleep in *peace*, for you alone, O Lord, make me dwell in safety.

—Psalm 4:6–8

YOU NEED ME EVERY MOMENT. Your awareness of your constant need for Me is your greatest strength. Your neediness, properly handled, is a link to My Presence. However, there are pitfalls that you must be on guard against: self-pity, self-preoccupation, giving up. Your inadequacy presents you with a continual choice—deep dependence on Me or despair. The emptiness you feel within will be filled either with problems or with My Presence. Make Me central in your consciousness by *praying continually*: simple, short prayers flowing out of the present moment. Use My Name liberally, to remind you of My Presence. *Keep on asking and you will receive, so that your gladness may be full and complete.*

PSALM 86:7; 1 THESSALONIANS 5:17; JOHN 16:24 AMP

In the day of my

trouble

I will call to you,

for you will

answer me.

—Psalm 86:7

May the God of hope fill you with all joy and peace as you trust in him, so that you may overflow with hope by the power of the Holy Spirit.

—Romans 15:13

LET ME FILL YOU with My Love, Joy, and Peace. These are Glory-gifts, flowing from My living Presence. Though you are an *earthen vessel*, I designed you to be filled with heavenly contents. Your weakness is not a deterrent to being filled with My Spirit; on the contrary, it provides an opportunity for My Power to shine forth more brightly.

As you go through this day, trust Me to provide the strength you need moment by moment. Don't waste energy wondering whether you are adequate for today's journey. My Spirit within you is more than sufficient to handle whatever this day may bring. That is the basis for your confidence! *In quietness* (spending time alone with Me) *and confident trust* (relying on My sufficiency) *is your strength*.

2 CORINTHIANS 4:7 NASB;
EPHESIANS 3:16; ISAIAH 30:15

I pray that out of his

glorious

riches he may

strengthen you with

power

through his Spirit in

your inner being.

—Ephesians 3:16

I AM *CHRIST IN YOU, the hope of Glory.* The One who walks beside you, holding you by your hand, is the same One who lives within you. This is a deep, unfathomable mystery. You and I are intertwined in an intimacy involving every fiber of your being. The Light of My Presence shines within you, as well as upon you. I am in you, and you are in Me; therefore nothing in heaven or on earth can separate you from Me!

As you sit quietly in My Presence, your awareness of My Life within you is heightened. This produces the *Joy of the Lord, which is your strength. I, the God of hope, fill you with all Joy and Peace as you trust in Me, so that you may bubble over with hope by the power of the Holy Spirit.*

COLOSSIANS 1:27; ISAIAH 42:6;
NEHEMIAH 8:10; ROMANS 15:13 AMP

"I, the LORD, have called you in

righteousness;

I will take hold of your hand.

I will keep you and will make

you to be a covenant for

the people and a *light*

for the Gentiles."

—ISAIAH 42:6

YOU ARE MY BELOVED CHILD. *I chose you before the foundation of the world*, to walk with Me along paths designed uniquely for you. Concentrate on keeping in step with Me instead of trying to anticipate My plans for you. If you trust that My plans are *to prosper you and not to harm you*, you can relax and enjoy the present moment.

Your hope and your future are rooted in heaven, where eternal ecstasy awaits you. Nothing can rob you of your inheritance of unimaginable riches and well-being. Sometimes I grant you glimpses of your glorious future, to encourage you and spur you on. But your main focus should be staying close to Me. I set the pace in keeping with your needs and My purposes.

EPHESIANS 1:4 NASB; PROVERBS 16:9;
JEREMIAH 29:11; EPHESIANS 1:13–14

And you also were included in Christ when you heard the word of *truth*, the gospel of your salvation. Having *believed*, you were marked in him with a seal, the promised Holy Spirit, who is a deposit guaranteeing our inheritance until the *redemption* of those who are God's possession—to the praise of his glory.

—EPHESIANS 1:13–14

YOUR LONGING for heaven is good because it is an extension of your yearning for Me. The hope of heaven is meant to strengthen and encourage you, filling you with wondrous Joy. Many Christians have misunderstood this word *hope*, believing that it denotes wishful thinking. Nothing could be further from the truth! As soon as I became your Savior, heaven became your ultimate destination. The phrase *hope of heaven* highlights the benefits you can enjoy even while remaining on earth. This hope keeps you spiritually alive during dark times of adversity; it brightens your path and heightens your awareness of My Presence. My desire is *that you may overflow with hope by the power of the Holy Spirit.*

ROMANS 8:23–25; HEBREWS 6:18–19; ROMANS 15:13

For in this *hope* we were saved. But hope that is seen is no hope at all. Who hopes for what he already has? But if we hope for what we do not yet have, we *wait* for it patiently.

—ROMANS 8:24-25

DO NOT LONG FOR THE ABSENCE of problems in your life. That is an unrealistic goal since *in this world you will have trouble.* You have an eternity of problem-free living reserved for you in heaven. Rejoice in that inheritance, which no one can take away from you, but do not seek your heaven on earth.

Begin each day anticipating problems, asking Me to equip you for whatever difficulties you will encounter. The best equipping is My living Presence, *My hand that never lets go of yours.* Discuss everything with Me. Take a lighthearted view of trouble, seeing it as a challenge that you and I together can handle. Remember that I am on your side, and *I have overcome the world.*

JOHN 16:13; ISAIAH 41:13; PHILIPPIANS 4:13

"For I am the Lord,

your God, who takes

hold of your right

hand and says to you,

Do not fear; I will

help you."

—Isaiah 41:13

Let us hold unswervingly to the hope we profess, for he who promised is faithful.

—Hebrews 10:23

TRY TO VIEW EACH DAY as an adventure, carefully planned out by your Guide. Instead of staring into the day that is ahead of you, attempting to program it according to your will, be attentive to Me and to all I have prepared for you. Thank Me for this day of life, recognizing that it is a precious, unrepeatable gift. Trust that I am with you each moment, whether you sense My Presence or not. A thankful, trusting attitude helps you to see events in your life from My perspective.

A life lived close to Me will never be dull or predictable. Expect each day to contain surprises! Resist your tendency to search for the easiest route through the day. Be willing to follow wherever I lead. No matter how steep or treacherous the path before you, the safest place to be is by My side.

PSALM 118:24 NKJV; ISAIAH 41:10; 1 PETER 2:21

To this you were called,

because *Christ*

suffered for you,

leaving you an

example,

that you should

follow in his steps.

—1 Peter 2:21

THERE IS NO PLACE so desolate that you cannot find Me there. When Hagar fled from her mistress, Sarah, into the wilderness, she thought she was utterly alone and forsaken. But Hagar encountered Me in that desolate place. There she addressed Me as *the Living One who sees me*. Through that encounter with My Presence, she gained courage to return to her mistress.

No set of circumstances could ever isolate you from My loving Presence. Not only do I see you always, I see you as a redeemed saint, gloriously radiant in My righteousness. That is why *I take great delight in you and rejoice over you with singing!*

GENESIS 16:13–14 AMP;
PSALM 139:7–10; ZEPHANIAH 3:17

Where can I go from your Spirit? Where can I flee from your presence? If I go up to the *heavens*, you are there; if I make my bed in the depths, you are there. If I rise on the wings of the dawn, if I settle on the far side of the sea, even there your hand will *guide* me, your right hand will hold me fast.

—Psalm 139:7–10

LET ME HELP YOU get through this day. There are many possible paths to travel between your getting up in the morning and your lying down at night. Stay alert to the many choice-points along the way, being continually aware of My Presence. You will get through this day one way or the other. One way is to moan and groan, stumbling along with shuffling feet. This will get you to the end of the day eventually, but there is a better way. You can choose to walk with Me along the path of Peace, leaning on Me as much as you need. There will still be difficulties along the way, but you can face them confidently in My strength. Thank Me for each problem you encounter, and watch to see how I transform trials into blessings.

1 CORINTHIANS 10:10; LUKE 1:79; 2 SAMUEL 22:29–30

You are my lamp, O LORD;

the LORD turns my darkness

into *light*. With your

help I can advance against

a troop; with my *God*

I can scale a wall.

—2 SAMUEL 22:29-30

Relax in My healing Presence. As you spend time with Me, your thoughts tend to jump ahead to today's plans and problems. Bring your mind back to Me for refreshment and renewal. Let the Light of My Presence soak into you as you focus your thoughts on Me. Thus I equip you to face whatever the day brings. This sacrifice of time pleases Me and strengthens you. Do not skimp on our time together. Resist the clamor of tasks waiting to be done. *You have chosen what is better, and it will not be taken away from you.*

PSALM 89:15; PSALM 105:4; LUKE 10:39–42

Blessed are those

who have learned

to acclaim you,

who walk in the

light of your

presence, O LORD.

—PSALM 89:15

WHEN THINGS SEEM to be going all wrong, stop and affirm your trust in Me. Calmly bring these matters to Me, and leave them in My capable hands. Then, simply do the next thing. Stay in touch with Me through thankful, trusting prayers, resting in My sovereign control. Rejoice in Me—exult in the God of your salvation! As you trust in Me, *I make your feet like the feet of a deer. I enable you to walk and make progress upon your high places of trouble, suffering, or responsibility.*

JOB 13:15 NKJV; PSALM 18:33; HABAKKUK 3:17–19 AMP

He makes my feet

like the feet of a deer;

he *enables*

me to stand on the

heights.

—Psalm 18:33

Even the youths shall faint and be weary, and the young men shall utterly fall, but those who wait on the LORD shall renew their strength; they shall mount up with wings like eagles, they shall run and not be weary, they shall walk and not faint.

—Isaiah 40:30–31 NKJV

DO NOT BE DISCOURAGED by the difficulty of keeping your focus on Me. I know that your heart's desire is to be aware of My Presence continually. This is a lofty goal; you aim toward it but never fully achieve it in this life. Don't let feelings of failure weigh you down. Instead, try to see yourself as I see you. First of all, I am delighted by your deep desire to walk closely with Me through your life. I am pleased each time you initiate communication with Me. In addition, I notice the progress you have made since you first resolved to live in My Presence.

When you realize that your mind has wandered away from Me, don't be alarmed or surprised. You live in a world that has been rigged to distract you. Each time you plow your way through the massive distractions to communicate with Me, you achieve a victory. Rejoice in these tiny triumphs, and they will increasingly light up your days.

ROMANS 8:33–34; HEBREWS 4:14–16

Who will bring any charge
against those whom God
has chosen? It is God who
justifies. Who
is he that condemns?
Christ Jesus, who died—
more than that, who was
raised to life—is at
the right hand of God and
is also interceding for us.

—Romans 8:33–34

REST IN MY PRESENCE WHEN you need refreshment. Resting is not necessarily idleness, as people often perceive it. When you relax in My company, you are demonstrating trust in Me. *Trust* is a rich word, laden with meaning and direction for your life. I want you to *lean on, trust, and be confident in Me.* When you lean on Me for support, I delight in your trusting confidence.

Many people turn away from Me when they are exhausted. They associate Me with duty and diligence, so they try to hide from My Presence when they need a break from work. How this saddens Me! As I spoke through My prophet Isaiah: *In returning to Me and resting in Me you shall be saved; in quietness and trust shall be your strength.*

PSALM 91:1; PROVERBS 3:5 AMP; ISAIAH 30:15 AMP

He who dwells in the

shelter

of the Most High

will rest in the

shadow of the

Almighty.

—Psalm 91:1

THE WORLD IS TOO MUCH WITH YOU, My child. Your mind leaps from problem to problem to problem, tangling your thoughts in anxious knots. When you think like that, you leave Me out of your worldview and your mind becomes darkened. Though I yearn to help, I will not violate your freedom. I stand silently in the background of your mind, waiting for you to remember that I am with you.

When you turn from your problems to My Presence, your load is immediately lighter. Circumstances may not have changed, but we carry your burdens together. Your compulsion to "fix" everything gives way to deep, satisfying connection with Me. Together we can handle whatever this day brings.

ISAIAH 41:10; ZEPHANIAH 3:17; PSALM 34:19

A *righteous* man

may have many troubles,

but the Lord

delivers

him from them all.

—Psalm 34:19

RELAX IN *MY EVERLASTING ARMS.* Your weakness is an opportunity to grow strong in awareness of My Almighty Presence. When your energy fails you, do not look inward and lament the lack you find there. Look to Me and My sufficiency; rejoice in My radiant riches that are abundantly available to help you.

Go gently through this day, leaning on Me and enjoying My Presence. Thank Me for your neediness, which is building trust-bonds between us. If you look back on your journey thus far, you can see that days of extreme weakness have been some of your most precious times. Memories of these days are richly interwoven with golden strands of My intimate Presence.

DEUTERONOMY 33:27; ROMANS 8:26; PSALM 27:13–14

I am still

confident

of this: I will see the goodness

of the LORD in the land of

the living. Wait for the LORD;

be *strong* and take

heart and wait for the LORD.

—PSALM 27:13–14

WAITING, TRUSTING, AND HOPING are intricately connected, like golden strands interwoven to form a strong chain. Trusting is the central strand because it is the response from My children that I desire the most. Waiting and hoping embellish the central strand and strengthen the chain that connects you to Me. Waiting for Me to work, with your eyes on Me, is evidence that you really do trust Me. If you mouth the words "I trust You" while anxiously trying to make things go your way, your words ring hollow. Hoping is future-directed, connecting you to your inheritance in heaven. However, the benefits of hope fall fully on you in the present.

Because you are Mine, you don't just pass time in your waiting. You can wait expectantly, in hopeful trust. Keep your "antennae" out to pick up even the faintest glimmer of My Presence.

JOHN 14:1; PSALM 27:14; HEBREWS 6:18–20

"Do not let your

hearts be troubled.

Trust in God;

trust also in me."

—John 14:1

In the same way, the Spirit helps us in our weakness. We do not know what we ought to pray for, but the Spirit himself intercedes for us with groans that words cannot express.

—Romans 8:26

I AM WITH YOU, watching over you constantly. I am Immanuel (*God with you*); My Presence enfolds you in radiant Love. Nothing, including the brightest blessings and the darkest trials, can separate you from Me. Some of My children find Me more readily during dark times, when difficulties force them to depend on Me. Others feel closer to Me when their lives are filled with good things. They respond with thanksgiving and praise, thus opening wide the door to My Presence.

I know precisely what you need to draw nearer to Me. Go through each day looking for what I have prepared for you. Accept every event as My hand-tailored provision for your needs. When you view your life this way, the most reasonable response is to be thankful. Do not reject any of My gifts; find Me in every situation.

MATTHEW 1:23; PSALM 34:5; COLOSSIANS 2:6–7

So then, just as you *received* Christ Jesus as Lord, continue to live in him, *rooted* and built up in him, strengthened in the faith as you were taught, and overflowing with *thankfulness*.

—Colossians 2:6-7

LEAVE OUTCOMES UP TO ME. Follow Me wherever I lead, without worrying about how it will all turn out. Think of your life as an adventure, with Me as your Guide and Companion. Live in the *now*, concentrating on staying in step with Me. When our path leads to a cliff, be willing to climb it with My help. When we come to a resting place, take time to be refreshed in My Presence. Enjoy the rhythm of life lived close to Me.

You already know the ultimate destination of your journey: your entrance into heaven. So keep your focus on the path just before you, leaving outcomes up to Me.

JOHN 10:4; PSALM 27:13–14; EXODUS 15:13

"When he has *brought* out all his own, he goes on ahead of them, and his sheep *follow* him because they know his voice."

—John 10:4

THIS IS THE DAY THAT I HAVE MADE. Rejoice and be glad in it. Begin the day with open hands of faith, ready to receive all that I am pouring into this brief portion of your life. Be careful not to complain about anything, even the weather, since I am the Author of your circumstances. The best way to handle unwanted situations is to thank Me for them. This act of faith frees you from resentment and frees Me to work My ways into the situation, so that good emerges from it.

To find Joy in this day, you must live within its boundaries. I knew what I was doing when I divided time into twenty-four-hour segments. I understand human frailty, and I know that you can bear the weight of only one day at a time. Do not worry about tomorrow or get stuck in the past. There is abundant Life in My Presence today.

PSALM 118:24; PHILIPPIANS 3:13–14; HEBREWS 3:13

This is the day the

Lord has *made*;

let us rejoice and be

glad in it.

—Psalm 118:24

THANK ME for the conditions that are requiring you to *be still*. Do not spoil these quiet hours by wishing them away, waiting impatiently to be active again. Some of the greatest works in My kingdom have been done from sickbeds and prison cells. Instead of resenting the limitations of a weakened body, search for My way in the midst of these very circumstances. Limitations can be liberating when your strongest desire is living close to Me.

Quietness and trust enhance your awareness of My Presence with you. Do not despise these simple ways of serving Me. Although you feel cut off from the activity of the world, your quiet trust makes a powerful statement in spiritual realms. *My Strength and Power show themselves most effective in weakness.*

ZECHARIAH 2:13; ISAIAH 30:15;
2 CORINTHIANS 12:9 AMP

This is what the Sovereign Lord, the Holy One of Israel, says: "In *repentance* and rest is your salvation, in quietness and trust is your *strength*."

—Isaiah 30:15

I AM A GOD of both intricate detail and overflowing abundance. When you entrust the details of your life to Me, you are surprised by how thoroughly I answer your petitions. I take pleasure in hearing your prayers, so feel free to bring Me all your requests. The more you pray, the more answers you can receive. Best of all, your faith is strengthened as you see how precisely I respond to your specific prayers.

Because I am infinite in all My ways, you need not fear that I will run out of resources. *Abundance* is at the very heart of who I AM. Come to Me in joyful expectation of receiving all you need—and sometimes much more! I delight in showering blessings on My beloved children. Come to Me with open hands and heart, ready to receive all I have for you.

PSALM 36:7–9; PSALM 132:15; JOHN 6:12–13

"I will *bless*

her with

abundant

provisions; her poor will I

satisfy

with food."

—PSALM 132:15

I can do everything through him who gives me strength.

—*Philippians 4:13*

DO NOT BE SURPRISED by the fiery attacks on your mind. When you struggle to find Me and to live in My Peace, don't let discouragement set in. You are engaged in massive warfare, spiritually speaking. The evil one abhors your closeness to Me, and his demonic underlings are determined to destroy our intimacy. When you find yourself in the thick of battle, call upon My Name: "Jesus, help me!" At that instant, the battle becomes Mine; your role is simply to trust Me as I fight for you.

My Name, properly used, has unlimited Power to bless and protect. At the end of time, *every knee will bow (in heaven, on earth, and under the earth) when My Name is proclaimed*. People who have used "Jesus" as a shoddy swear word will fall down in terror on that awesome day. But all those who have drawn near Me through trustingly uttering My Name will be filled with *inexpressible and glorious Joy*. This is your great hope as you await My return.

EPHESIANS 6:12; PHILIPPIANS 2:9–10; 1 PETER 1:8–9

Though you have not seen him, you *love* him; and even though you do not see him now, you believe in him and are *filled* with an inexpressible and glorious joy, for you are receiving the goal of your *faith*, the salvation of your souls.

—1 Peter 1:8-9

I WANT YOU TO EXPERIENCE the riches of your salvation: the Joy of being loved constantly and perfectly. You make a practice of judging yourself based on how you look or behave or feel. If you like what you see in the mirror, you feel a bit more worthy of My Love. When things are going smoothly and your performance seems adequate, you find it easier to believe you are My beloved child. When you feel discouraged, you tend to look inward so you can correct whatever is wrong.

Instead of trying to "fix" yourself, *fix your gaze on Me, the Lover of your soul.* Rather than using your energy to judge yourself, redirect it to praising Me. Remember that I see you clothed in My righteousness, radiant in My perfect Love.

EPHESIANS 2:7–8; HEBREWS 3:1; PSALM 34:5

Those who look to him are

radiant;

their faces are never

covered with shame.

—Psalm 34:5

TRUST ME AND REFUSE TO WORRY, for *I am your Strength and Song*. You are feeling wobbly this morning, looking at difficult times looming ahead, measuring them against your own strength. However, they are not today's tasks—or even tomorrow's. So leave them in the future and come home to the present, where you will find Me waiting for you. Since *I am your Strength*, I can empower you to handle each task as it comes. Because *I am your Song*, I can give you Joy as you work alongside Me.

Keep bringing your mind back to the present moment. Among all My creatures, only humans can anticipate future events. This ability is a blessing, but it becomes a curse whenever it is misused. If you use your magnificent mind to worry about tomorrow, you cloak yourself in dark unbelief. However, when the hope of heaven fills your thoughts, the Light of My Presence envelops you. Though heaven is future, it is also present tense. As you walk in the Light with Me, you have one foot on earth and one foot in heaven.

EXODUS 15:2; 2 CORINTHIANS 10:5; HEBREWS 10:23

The LORD is my

strength

and my song; he has

become my salvation.

He is my God, and I will

praise him,

my father's God, and

I will exalt him.

—EXODUS 15:2

WALK BY FAITH, NOT BY SIGHT. As you take steps of faith, depending on Me, I will show you how much I can do for you. If you live your life too safely, you will never know the thrill of seeing Me work through you. When I gave you My Spirit, I empowered you to live beyond your natural ability and strength. That's why it is so wrong to measure your energy level against the challenges ahead of you. The issue is not your strength but Mine, which is limitless. By walking close to Me, you can accomplish My purposes in My strength.

2 CORINTHIANS 5:7 NKJV;

GALATIANS 5:25; PSALM 59:16–17

But I will sing of your *strength*, in the morning I will sing of your love; for you are my fortress, my refuge in times of trouble. O my Strength, I sing praise to you; you, O God, are my *fortress*, my loving God.

—PSALM 59:16–17

I AM WITH YOU. These four words are like a safety net, protecting you from falling into despair. Because you are human, you will always have ups and downs in your life experience. But the promise of My Presence limits how far down you can go. Sometimes you may feel as if you are in a free fall when people or things you had counted on let you down. Yet as soon as you remember that *I am with you,* your perspective changes radically. Instead of bemoaning your circumstances, you can look to Me for help. You recall that not only am I with you; *I am holding you by your right hand. I guide you with My counsel, and afterward I will take you into Glory.* This is exactly the perspective you need: the reassurance of My Presence and the glorious hope of heaven.

ZEPHANIAH 3:17; PSALM 73:23–26

Yet I am always with you; you hold me by my right hand. You *guide* me with your counsel, and afterward you will take me into glory. Whom have I in heaven but you? And earth has nothing I desire besides you. My flesh and my heart may fail, but God is the *strength* of my heart and my portion forever.

—Psalm 73:23–26

How priceless is your unfailing love! Both high and low among men find refuge in the shadow of your wings. They feast on the abundance of your house; you give them drink from your river of delights. For with you is the fountain of life; in your light we see light.

—Psalm 36:7–9

GROW STRONG in the Light of My Presence. Your weakness does not repel Me. On the contrary, it attracts My Power, which is always available to flow into a yielded heart. Do not condemn yourself for your constant need of help. Instead, come to Me with your gaping neediness; let the Light of My Love fill you.

A yielded heart does not whine or rebel when the going gets rough. It musters the courage to thank Me even during hard times. Yielding yourself to My will is ultimately an act of trust. *In quietness and trust is your strength.*

PSALM 116:5–7; EPHESIANS 5:20; ISAIAH 30:15

The LORD is gracious and

righteous; our God

is full of compassion. The LORD

protects the simplehearted;

when I was in great need,

he saved me. Be at *rest*

once more, O my soul, for the

LORD has been good to you.

—PSALM 116:5–7

IN A WORLD OF UNRELENTING CHANGES, I am the One who never changes. *I am the Alpha and the Omega, the First and the Last, the Beginning and the End.* Find in Me the stability for which you have yearned.

I created a beautifully ordered world: one that reflects My perfection. Now, however, the world is under the bondage of sin and evil. Every person on the planet faces gaping jaws of uncertainty. The only antidote to this poisonous threat is drawing closer to Me. In My Presence you can face uncertainty with perfect Peace.

REVELATION 22:13; ROMANS 5:12; JOHN 16:33 AMP

"I am the Alpha

and the Omega,

the *First*

and the Last,

the Beginning

and the *End*."

—REVELATION 22:13

TRUST ME, and don't be afraid. I want you to view trials as exercises designed to develop your trust-muscles. You live in the midst of fierce spiritual battles, and fear is one of Satan's favorite weapons. When you start to feel afraid, affirm your trust in Me. Speak out loud, if circumstances permit. *Resist the devil in My Name, and he will slink away from you.* Refresh yourself in My holy Presence. Speak or sing praises to Me, and My Face will shine radiantly upon you.

Remember that *there is no condemnation for those who belong to Me.* You have been judged NOT GUILTY for all eternity. *Trust Me, and don't be afraid; for I am your Strength, Song, and Salvation.*

JAMES 4:7; ROMANS 8:1–2; ISAIAH 12:2

Submit

yourselves, then,

to God.

Resist

the devil,

and he will

flee from you.

—JAMES 4:7

COME TO ME with empty hands and an open heart, ready to receive abundant blessings. I know the depth and breadth of your neediness. Your life-path has been difficult, draining you of strength. Come to Me for nurture. Let Me fill you up with My Presence: I in you, and you in Me.

My Power flows most freely into weak ones aware of their need for Me. Faltering steps of dependence are not lack of faith; they are links to My Presence.

JOHN 17:20–23; ISAIAH 40:29–31

"My *prayer* is not for them alone. I pray also for those who will *believe* in me through their message, that all of them may be *one*, Father, just as you are in me and I am in you."

—John 17:20-21

IT'S ALL RIGHT TO BE HUMAN. When your mind wanders while you are praying, don't be surprised or upset. Simply return your attention to Me. Share a secret smile with Me, knowing that I understand. Rejoice in My Love for you, which has no limits or conditions. Whisper My Name in loving contentment, assured that *I will never leave you or forsake you.* Intersperse these peaceful interludes abundantly throughout your day. This practice will enable you to attain *a quiet and gentle spirit,* which is pleasing to Me.

As you live in close contact with Me, the Light of My Presence filters through you to bless others. Your weakness and woundedness are the openings through which *the Light of the knowledge of My Glory* shines forth. *My strength and power show themselves most effective in your weakness.*

DEUTERONOMY 31:6; 1 PETER 3:4;
2 CORINTHIANS 4:6–7; 2 CORINTHIANS 12:9 AMP

Instead, it should be that of

your inner self, the unfading

beauty of a gentle and

quiet spirit, which is of great

worth in God's sight.

—1 PETER 3:4

In your unfailing love you will lead the people you have redeemed. In your strength you will guide them to your holy dwelling.

—Exodus 15:13

Trust Me and don't be afraid, for I am your Strength and Song. Think what it means to have Me as your Strength. I spoke the universe into existence; My Power is absolutely unlimited! Human weakness, consecrated to Me, is like a magnet, drawing My Power into your neediness. However, fear can block the flow of My Strength into you. Instead of trying to fight your fears, concentrate on trusting Me. When you relate to Me in confident trust, there is no limit to how much I can strengthen you.

Remember that I am also your Song. I want you to share My Joy, living in conscious awareness of My Presence. Rejoice as we journey together toward heaven; join Me in singing My Song.

Isaiah 12:2–3; Psalm 56:3 nkjv; Psalm 21:6

"Surely God is my salvation; I will *trust* and not be afraid. The LORD, the LORD, is my *strength* and my song; he has become my salvation." With joy you will draw water from the wells of salvation.

—ISAIAH 12:2–3

I AM PLEASED WITH YOU, MY CHILD. Allow
yourself to become fully aware of My pleasure shining
upon you. You don't have to perform well in order to
receive My Love. In fact, a performance focus will pull
you away from Me, toward some sort of Pharisaism.
This can be a subtle form of idolatry: worshiping your
own good works. It can also be a source of deep discouragement when your works don't measure up to your
expectations.

Shift your focus from your performance to My
radiant Presence. The Light of My Love shines on you
continually, regardless of your feelings or behavior. Your
responsibility is to be receptive to this unconditional
Love. Thankfulness and trust are your primary recep-
tors. Thank Me for everything; *trust in Me at all times.*
These simple disciplines will keep you open to My loving Presence.

EPHESIANS 2:8–9; EPHESIANS 3:16–19; PSALM 62:8

For it is by grace

you have been

saved,

through faith—and this

not from yourselves,

it is the *gift* of God—

not by works, so that

no one can boast.

—Ephesians 2:8–9

LET MY LOVE STREAM THROUGH YOU, washing away fear and distrust. A trusting response includes Me in your thoughts as you consider strategies to deal with a situation. My continual Presence is a promise, guaranteeing that you never have to face anything alone. My children teethe on the truth that I am always with them, yet they stumble around in a stupor, unaware of My loving Presence all around them. How that grieves Me!

When you walk through a day in trusting dependence on Me, My aching heart is soothed. Gently bring your attention back to Me whenever it wanders away. I look for persistence—rather than perfection—in your walk with Me.

PSALM 52:8; DEUTERONOMY 31:6; EPHESIANS 4:30

But I am like an olive tree

flourishing

in the house of God;

I trust in God's unfailing

love

for ever and ever.

—Psalm 52:8

I MEET YOU in the stillness of your soul. It is there that I seek to commune with you. A person who is open to My Presence is exceedingly precious to Me. My eyes *search to and fro throughout the earth*, looking for one whose heart is seeking Me. I see you trying to find Me; our mutual search results in joyful fulfillment.

Stillness of soul is increasingly rare in this world addicted to noise and speed. I am pleased with your desire to create a quiet space where you and I can meet. Don't be discouraged by the difficulty of achieving this goal. I monitor all your efforts and am blessed by each of your attempts to seek My Face.

ZECHARIAH 2:13; 2 CHRONICLES 16:9 NKJV;
PSALM 23:2–3 NKJV

"Be still before

the LORD, all

mankind,

because he has

roused himself from his

holy dwelling."

—ZECHARIAH 2:13

BE STILL IN THE LIGHT of My Presence while I communicate Love to you. There is no force in the universe as powerful as My Love. You are constantly aware of limitations: your own and others'. But there is no limit to My Love; it fills all of space, time, and eternity.

Now you see through a glass, darkly, but someday you will see Me face to Face. Then you will be able to experience fully *how wide and long and high and deep is My Love for you.* If you were to experience that now, you would be overwhelmed to the point of feeling crushed. But you have an eternity ahead of you, absolutely guaranteed, during which you can enjoy My Presence in unrestricted ecstasy. For now, the knowledge of My loving Presence is sufficient to carry you through each day.

1 CORINTHIANS 13:12 KJV; EPHESIANS 3:16–19

For now we *see* through

a glass, darkly; but then face

to face: now I know in part;

but then shall I *know*

even as also I am known.

—1 Corinthians 13:12 KJV

But in keeping with his promise we are looking forward to a new heaven and a new earth, the home of righteousness.

—2 Peter 3:13

APPROACH EACH NEW DAY with desire to find Me. Before you get out of bed, I have already been working to prepare the path that will get you through this day. There are hidden treasures strategically placed along the way. Some of the treasures are trials, designed to shake you free from earth-shackles. Others are blessings that reveal My Presence: sunshine, flowers, birds, friendships, answered prayer. I have not abandoned this sin-wracked world; I am still richly present in it.

Search for deep treasure as you go through this day. You will find Me all along the way.

PROVERBS 16:9 AMP; COLOSSIANS 2:2–3; ISAIAH 33:6

He will be the sure

foundation

for your times, a rich store

of salvation and wisdom and

knowledge;

the fear of the Lord is the

key to this *treasure*.

—ISAIAH 33:6

I AM TRAINING YOU IN STEADINESS. Too many things interrupt your awareness of Me. I know that you live in a world of sight and sound, but you must not be a slave to those stimuli. Awareness of Me can continue in all circumstances, no matter what happens. This is the steadiness I desire for you.

Don't let unexpected events throw you off course. Rather, respond calmly and confidently, remembering that I am with you. As soon as something grabs your attention, talk with Me about it. Thus I share your joys and your problems; I help you cope with whatever is before you. This is how I live in you and work through you. This is the way of Peace.

PSALM 112:7; 1 THESSALONIANS 5:17 AMP;
ISAIAH 41:10 NKJV

He will have

no fear

of bad news;

his heart is

steadfast,

trusting in the LORD.

—PSALM 112:7

HOPE IS A GOLDEN CORD connecting you to heaven. This cord helps you hold your head up high, even when multiple trials are buffeting you. I never leave your side, and I never let go of your hand. But without the cord of hope, your head may slump and your feet may shuffle as you journey uphill with Me. Hope lifts your perspective from your weary feet to the glorious view you can see from the high road. You are reminded that the road we're traveling together is ultimately a highway to heaven. When you consider this radiant destination, the roughness or smoothness of the road ahead becomes much less significant. I am training you to hold in your heart a dual focus: My continual Presence and the hope of heaven.

ROMANS 12:12; 1 THESSALONIANS 5:8;
HEBREWS 6:18–19

But since we

belong to the day,

let us be self-controlled,

putting on *faith*

and love as a breastplate,

and the *hope* of

salvation as a helmet.

—1 Thessalonians 5:8

WELCOME CHALLENGING TIMES as opportunities to trust Me. You have Me beside you and My Spirit within you, so no set of circumstances is too much for you to handle. When the path before you is dotted with difficulties, beware of measuring your strength against those challenges. That calculation is certain to riddle you with anxiety. Without Me, you wouldn't make it past the first hurdle!

The way to walk through demanding days is to grip My hand tightly and stay in close communication with Me. Let your thoughts and spoken words be richly flavored with trust and thankfulness. Regardless of the day's problems, *I can keep you in perfect Peace* as you stay close to Me.

JAMES 1:2; PHILIPPIANS 4:13 NKJV; ISAIAH 26:3

You will keep in

perfect peace

him whose mind is

steadfast, because he

trusts in you.

—Isaiah 26:3

YOUR NEEDS AND MY RICHES are a perfect fit. I never meant for you to be self-sufficient. Instead, I designed you to need Me not only for daily bread but also for fulfillment of deep yearnings. I carefully crafted your longings and feelings of incompleteness to point you to Me. Therefore, do not try to bury or deny these feelings. Beware also of trying to pacify these longings with lesser gods: people, possessions, power.

Come to Me in all your neediness, with defenses down and with desire to be blessed. As you spend time in My Presence, your deepest longings are fulfilled. Rejoice in your neediness, which enables you to find intimate completion in Me.

PHILIPPIANS 4:19; COLOSSIANS 2:2–3;
PSALM 84:11–12 NKJV

And my God

will meet all your

needs according

to his glorious

riches

in Christ Jesus.

—Philippians 4:19

My purpose is that they may be encouraged in heart and united in love, so that they may have the full riches of complete understanding, in order that they may know the mystery of God, namely, Christ, in whom are hidden all the treasures of wisdom and knowledge.

—Colossians 2:2–3

LIVING IN DEPENDENCE ON ME is the way to enjoy abundant life. You are learning to appreciate tough times because they amplify your awareness of My Presence. Tasks that you used to dread are becoming rich opportunities to enjoy My closeness. When you feel tired, you remember that I am your Strength; you take pleasure in leaning on Me. I am pleased by your tendency to turn to Me more and more frequently, especially when you are alone.

When you are with other people, you often lose sight of My Presence. Your fear of displeasing people puts you in bondage to them, and they become your primary focus. When you realize this has happened, whisper My Name; this tiny act of trust brings Me to the forefront of your consciousness, where I belong. As you bask in the blessing of My nearness, My life can flow through you to others. This is abundant life!

PSALM 18:1–2; PROVERBS 29:25; JOHN 10:10 NKJV

I love you, O LORD, my *strength*. The LORD is my rock, my fortress and my *deliverer*; my God is my rock, in whom I take refuge. He is my shield and the horn of my salvation, my *stronghold*.

—PSALM 18:1–2

HEAVEN IS both present and future. As you walk along your life-path holding My hand, you are already in touch with the essence of heaven: nearness to Me. You can also find many hints of heaven along your pathway because the earth is radiantly alive with My Presence. Shimmering sunshine awakens your heart, gently reminding you of My brilliant Light. Birds and flowers, trees and skies evoke praises to My holy Name. Keep your eyes and ears fully open as you journey with Me.

At the end of your life-path is an entrance to heaven. Only I know when you will reach that destination, but I am preparing you for it each step of the way. The absolute certainty of your heavenly home gives you Peace and Joy to help you along your journey. You know that you will reach your home in My perfect timing: not one moment too soon or too late. Let the hope of heaven encourage you as you walk along the path of Life with Me.

1 CORINTHIANS 15:20–23; HEBREWS 6:19

We have this

hope as an anchor

for the soul, firm and

secure. It enters

the inner sanctuary

behind the curtain.

—Hebrews 6:19

IT IS GOOD THAT YOU RECOGNIZE YOUR WEAKNESS. That keeps you looking to Me, your Strength. Abundant life is not necessarily health and wealth; it is living in continual dependence on Me. Instead of trying to fit this day into a preconceived mold, relax and be on the lookout for what I am doing. This mind-set will free you to enjoy Me and to find what I have planned for you to do. This is far better than trying to make things go according to your own plan.

Don't take yourself so seriously. Lighten up and laugh with Me. You have Me on your side, so what are you worried about? I can equip you to do absolutely anything, as long as it is My will. The more difficult your day, the more I yearn to help you. Anxiety wraps you up in yourself, trapping you in your own thoughts. When you look to Me and whisper My Name, you break free and receive My help. Focus on Me, and you will find Peace in My Presence.

PHILIPPIANS 4:13 AMP; PROVERBS 17:22

A *cheerful* heart
is good medicine, but a
crushed *spirit*
dries up the bones.

—Proverbs 17:22

KEEP YOUR EYES ON ME! Waves of adversity are washing over you, and you feel tempted to give up. As your circumstances consume more and more of your attention, you are losing sight of Me. Yet *I am with you always, holding you by your right hand.* I am fully aware of your situation, *and I will not allow you to be tempted beyond what you are able to bear.*

Your gravest danger is worrying about tomorrow. If you try to carry tomorrow's burdens today, you will stagger under the load and eventually fall flat. You must discipline yourself to live within the boundaries of today. It is in the present moment that I walk close to you, helping you carry your burdens. Keep your focus on My Presence in the present.

PSALM 73:23; 1 CORINTHIANS 10:13; HEBREWS 3:13

No temptation has seized you

except what is common to man.

And God is *faithful*;

he will not let you be tempted

beyond what you can bear. But

when you are tempted, he will

also *provide* a way out

so that you can stand up under it.

—1 Corinthians 10:13

I AM ABLE to do far beyond all that you ask or imagine. Come to Me with positive expectations, knowing that there is no limit to what I can accomplish. Ask My Spirit to control your mind so that you can think great thoughts of Me. Do not be discouraged by the fact that many of your prayers are yet unanswered. Time is a trainer, teaching you to wait upon Me, to trust Me in the dark. The more extreme your circumstances, the more likely you are to see *My Power and Glory* at work in the situation. Instead of letting difficulties draw you into worrying, try to view them as setting the scene for My glorious intervention. Keep your eyes and your mind wide open to all that I am doing in your life.

EPHESIANS 3:20–21; ROMANS 8:6;

ISAIAH 40:30–31 NKJV

Now to him who is *able* to do immeasurably more than all we ask or imagine, according to his *power* that is at work within us, to him be glory in the church and in Christ Jesus throughout *all* generations, for ever and ever! Amen.

—Ephesians 3:20-21

*The LORD your God is with you,
he is mighty to save. He will take
great delight in you, he will quiet*

you with his love, he will rejoice over you with singing.

—Zephaniah 3:17